LET ME TELL YOU A STORY...

NYU ABU DHABI

Aiya Akilzhanova, Abdulla Al Hemeiri, Thais Alvarenga, Daniella Aruina, Elen Asatryan, Adi Baurzhanuly, Myriam Bekkoucha, Gabrielle Branche, Colin Campbell, Mariana Lugo Celedon, Harper Cho, Daniel De Beer, Uriel Dison, Sakura Grant, Julius Grüner, Dylan Herman, Tiffany Holung, Sofija Jancheska, Hannah Kasak-Gliboff, Michael Leo, Megan Marzolf, Abhay Menon, Eliza Mic, Maya Muwanga, Fatima Nadeem, Susanne Niemann, Andrijana Pejchinovska, Vera Petrova, Andrew Platonov, Zerina Rahic, Ania Rygielska, Sudiṭ K. Sahoo, Andres Lopez Schrader, Kacper Scibski, Elena Sepetovska, Alem Shaimardanov, Michael Shiloh, Penina Shtauber, Mayson Taylor, Bar Tenenbaum, Phil Wee, Cameron Wehr

This book was made possible by partnering with the Bronfman Center at New York University in collaboration with NYU Abu Dhabi, and the IACT program at Hillel International.

At Giant Story Press, we believe every person has a giant story to tell. We cater creative nonfiction writing workshops to groups, which concludes with the publication of a collection. If you would like to host a workshop with us, be in touch with Penina Shtauber at peninashtauber@gmail.com

ISBN 978-965-92757-3-1
First printing 2021

Who is wise? One who learns from every person.

— Ben Zoma, Ethics of the Fathers, 4:1

CONTENTS

Editor's Note

When we first emailed the NYU Abu Dhabi student body announcing that the Jewish Learning Fellowship (JLF) was coming to campus, we assumed it would gain moderate traction at best. We were, however, surprised and deeply moved when nearly one hundred students from across the world, many of whom having no prior exposure to Judaism, rushed to sign up for the first-ever class taught on Judaism at NYU Abu Dhabi. For the following ten weeks, the JLF cohort dove into rich discussions exploring questions of Judaism, Jewish culture, and philosophy together.

As facilitators, we prepared a syllabus of weekly themes and complementary readings for the ten-week course. What truly enriched our sessions, though, were the voices of our students. The inaugural NYU Abu Dhabi JLF cohort shared openly and honestly, approached new and complex topics with intentionality, and demonstrated empathy for one another.

It was through our rich discussions that this collection of stories was born. Let Me Tell You a Story... is a compilation of essays by our students reflecting on their growth throughout the JLF course. While our time in class may be over, this book serves as a special reminder of the openness, courage, and enthusiasm of our JLF cohort, for which we are deeply grateful.

Uriel Dison and Penina Shtauber

"Where are You From From?"
Tiffany A. Holung

"Your existence makes no sense, but it could be the start to end racism."

The first time I realized I was different, I was about ten years old. Don't get me wrong – we're all unique in our own special way – but when my 5th grade Social Studies teacher told me I could be the end to racism, I had no idea what she was talking about.

I grew up in a Jewish-Muslim household, but I went to Catholic school my entire life; you can simply call me the original Abrahamic Accord. To make things even more complicated, I have a half- Israeli half- Chinese Canadian father and a Lebanese mother. I never knew that was an issue as a child. I grew up in Jamaica, so race was never a huge deal as being Jamaican was a nationality rather than an ethnicity and that's all that mattered. Or at least that's what I was told. I never had to ever introduce myself saying, "Hi my name is Tiffany, and my father is Jewish-Chinese but he's Canadian on paper and my mother is Cuban-Lebanese but born and raised in Jamaica." I never ever had to say that until the day I began university, and someone asked me, "what am I?"

What am I? The question always made me uncomfortable. That and "where are you *from* from," always managed to strike a nerve I never knew existed.

Why does it matter?

Religion was never forced on me as a child. Understandably. What would you teach a child who had an atheist Jewish father and agnostic Muslim mother other than how to be a 'decent' human being? We were culturally Jewish-Muslim and even Christian. We celebrated my bat mitzvah and my brother had a brit as well as a bar mitzvah. Annually, we celebrate Eid, Hannukah, Christmas, Easter, Passover, Rosh Hashana, Ramadan, you name it, we celebrate it. Maybe it's an excuse to always host a party but the significance of these holidays and festivals were always acknowledged and taught as far back as I can remember.

That's what makes my relationship with God special. It was never forced – it was a choice. Even though I made a decision, the fundamental principles of each of the three religions serve as pillars which my life is dependent and based on.

You'll probably never find me in a mosque, synagogue or a church unless there's a special event happening or if someone invites me to go but that doesn't make my relationship with God any less than those who do.

So back to the question, what am I and where am I *from* from?

I'm Tiffany, I hold three passports, I speak five languages, and I'm human just like all of you.

Conversations Keep Me Going (Moving)
Andrés López Schrader

"Where do you see yourself in 5 years?"

We've all been asked this question. When I was finishing high school, the mere thought of constructing a hypothetical future version of myself got me instantly excited. Now, I am afraid that routine and loneliness will consume my life and the excitement will wither away.

I grew up in a homogenous white suburban neighborhood in Ohio surrounded by corn fields. The highlights of the year were refreshing water fights in the summer, corn mazes in the fall, first snowfall in the winter and colorful blooming gardens in the spring.

When I was 11, I transplanted my life and grew new roots in

Lima, Peru. Luckily for me I spoke Spanish before making the move, though my heavy American accent was a dead give-away that I wasn't a local. I started claiming my independence while living in Lima by testing my parent's limits every time I left the house. I learnt how to navigate the complex informal bus system, made friends with the shop owners on our suburban street and regularly ventured to the beach for sunset surfing.

Lima was another homogeneous community. This time, however, I was exposed to snippets of life outside my bubble through my mostly British teachers. My school strove to create "well-rounded citizens" through international education. For the most part I think they accomplished casting that mold onto most of their students, including myself.

The first time I was confronted with intense diversity it was the kaleidoscope of students that embarked on a 4-year adventure with me at NYU Abu Dhabi.

Intercultural curiosity is the defining feature of an NYU Abu Dhabi student. This curiosity breeds conversation. Ideas exchanged in the classroom, through essays, during debates, across dining tables, on the highline, under the palm trees, throughout taxi rides and at the beach. Wherever you look, you see ideas being shared. Whenever you listen, you hear thoughts in the air. When you first step foot on campus the socially active, constantly shifting environment can feel overwhelming. There's a level of caution you learn to live with in a place like this. The plethora of backgrounds and cultures we come from made it difficult to know what to say and what to do without offending anyone.

Eventually, it grew on me. People that are willing to entertain questions, no matter how big, small, complex or straightforward they may seem. How can we stop climate change? What is the purpose of life? Why do we speak different languages? Where did the first campus come from? I strongly connected with the environment created by people from all walks of life. The fear of offending diminished and eventually I even felt confident bouncing ideas off of the wide array of opinions available amongst my peers and friends. I reconsidered my internal truths – the preconceptions that had been handed down by my family.

Now I'm leaving this place. I'm leaving the community that runs on the communal act of sharing. No more spontaneous, organic late night conversations. But the lesson remains: it's easier to ride a bike when it's in motion. Keep reconsidering truths by discussing them with people around you.

I now realize how much I will miss this community and I truly appreciate the pleasure conversations provide for me.

In theory, interesting conversations can be fostered anywhere. But NYU Abu Dhabi has set an outstandingly high bar.

Eid Al-Adha, The Muslim Passover
Abdulla Saeed Alhemeiri

I woke up before the sunrise, filled with joy and excitement for the day. It is Eid Al-Adha, a day where we celebrate the submission of Prophet Abraham and his son to God. I went to pray in the mosque with my brother and returned home to find my family gathered. My mother, siblings, uncles, and aunts all greeting each other with a smile. We ate breakfast together and shared many stories. At 10:00 AM, I went outside with my uncle to perform a ritual. In Islam, we believe that God provided Abraham with a lamb to sacrifice instead of his son. Thus, my uncle sacrificed a sheep for the family to eat at lunch and sent me to distribute the rest for the needy people. I was given a few lamb parts in decorated bags to distribute around the neighborhood. It was a weary journey, but the smile on the faces of those that accepted the gifts wiped my exhaustion away.

I went back home and entered the Majlis, a sitting place for family members and visitors for chatting. In Majlis, the old spread their wisdom to the young. We sat and listened to many inspiring stories of how our grandfathers lived in the Arabian desert. They used to ride camels, plant their own food, and fight for their freedom. The most memorable story is of my maternal grandfather who was sent to Britain to study by an official order. After few hours, Me and my young relatives decided to wander around the neighborhood and have our share of stories. We usually talk about schools, football teams, and what we want to be when we grow up.

Later in the day, my family gathered in few cars and visited distant family members in a larger gathering. The moment I step out of the car and greet all my relatives is where the fun begins. As usual, we played video games, cards, and chit-chatted for few hours. Then, I gathered with my relatives to play football games in the imaginary field that we created. We set up goals by placing two shoes on each side and picture as a goal frame. We set our own rules offside, and we drew the field lines using our minds.

Fast forward to this semester, I decided to enroll in the Jewish Learning Fellowship because I believe that global unity starts when humans understand each other. I was eager to learn about the Jewish religion and culture firsthand. I was amused when I knew how Passover and Eid Al-Adha were conceptually similar. Passover is a celebration in Judaism of the Israelites liberation from Ancient Egypt. Jewish families gather for Passover seder, celebrate it with joy, and recite the Old Testament verses. Moreover, Many Jews sacrifice a lamb on the first day of Passover, which is similar to the Islamic sacrifice. Although the reasoning behind the Islamic and Jewish commemoration differs, I believe that the virtues of both celebrations are identical. The merit of sincere binding is the heart of every celebration. Nevertheless, I decided to research a story that binds Jews, Muslims, and Christians together. And I found that Abrahamic religions believe in the story of Abraham and the scarification of his son. Now imagine Muslims, Jews, and Christians sitting at one table commemorating this event with love and peace. Wouldn't that be pleasant?

It's Good To Be Home

Sakura Frances Grant

"Action!" I shout as I clap my hands together. I smile a wide smile at my little brother pointing the big Canon camera at me, thinking about what to say next.

"Hello! My name is S---ra and I'm from … well, I don't know!"

My parents chuckled as I giggled shyly at the camera and my brother behind it. But my eight-year-old self's artless statement encapsulated my sense of cultural confusion. I practically skipped over my name because I didn't know the right way to say it in English after being called by so many variations, and I didn't know where to say I was from. It was too confusing to tell people that my mom is Japanese, my dad is Kiwi, and I was born in Australia, but I live in Brazil or Singapore or Houston.

I understand; it confused me, too.

In a way, it was isolating: not knowing where to say I was from because I would overthink about the answer the person would want. Should I go with where I live or where my parents are from or what? I have big families in two completely different countries, yet I have lived in neither place. Generally, we go home to these families every one to three years, or whenever we can depending on where we live, so I have not had the chance to form deep connections or make friends in Japan or New Zealand. As I have grown and matured, I have come to be able to read when people are looking for my nationality or the place I call home, so I answer depending on that sense.

"Home" has never been constant for me, at least not for long. For a while, I envied those that had grown up in one place for their entire lives and were so sure of "home." They had grandparents living across the street from them, big family Christmases in their houses, and all fifteen of their extended family members at their graduation. So, my definition of home became the place where, when I was coming back from a trip, whether on a plane or car, I felt this sense of belonging and relief just as I was landing. Where I felt the comforting feeling of "it's good to be home" that many of us know. For the past few years, that place has been Houston, Texas, a place where I feel good to say I'm from and feel close to. Now that I am in college nowhere near home, it's even more comforting to have a home and routine to go back to at the end of the semester for a few weeks, like I finally have a constant.

Unfortunately, life does not stay easy forever, it is full of change and situations that will make you question a million things. Knowing that my family will be moving from

Houston to New Zealand this summer, during this whirlwind of a pandemic, when I cannot visit either place before the fall semester, I question where and when I will define my sense of home again. It feels strange to call Houston "home" after my family moves away because there will be nothing left for me there other than my friends and high school I left behind. It also feels odd to call New Zealand "home" because I have only been there a dozen or so times on vacations and have never truly lived there.

Thinking back to that video that I made all those years ago, I feel the same way as my eight-year-old self, but slightly less confused. However, I am twelve years older than I was, and I know for a fact that life just has to play itself out. Every confusing, complicated, and messy experience shapes you as a person and makes you all the more resilient. The best we can do is find comfort in discomfort until there is no need to anymore. What I have come to realize (with all the moving around and going to college abroad), more than anything, is that home truly is where the heart is, and that it is the people (friends and/or family), not only the place that makes a home—and you can have multiple!

The Storyteller and the Snake
Michael Leo

My grandfather is a storyteller. A good one too. He used to say that telling stories was the best way to keep our forefathers alive. "We die twice. The second time is the last time our name is spoken." He never elaborated, and I didn't care enough to try to make sense of it. But some things bothered me; why did he choose to tell depressing stories along with fun ones? Why did he always act like he was there when they happened? What possible purpose could reliving trauma serve?

I finally understood the day I killed a snake.

I had just turned 15, which meant I had permission to

drive outside his house in India. I was behind the wheel, my grandfather beside me; he was already grumbling at my erratic steering. Suddenly, he shouted: "SNAKE!" He pointed frantically somewhere to the left of the windscreen. It was a narrow road, I was focusing on too many things to realize what he had just yelled, and half a second later, I heard a thud outside the car.

I stopped immediately, as the full weight of what the sound meant slammed against my body. I unconsciously held on to the car for support as I walked to the back.

When I saw the snake I had run over, writhing and thrashing, I could almost hear it screaming. I experienced a sort of pitying awe, simultaneously feeling a sense of reverence and great remorse. Grandad told me to stay back, there was nothing we could do; I walked to the car and sat down in the passenger seat. My grandfather drove us back.

Throughout the ride he tried to console me; he told me it wasn't my fault, there was nothing I could have done, and now that I'd learned my lesson, I would be more careful. The entire time he spoke, all I could hear was the sickening 'thud'. All I saw was the snake's crushed, twisting body. The snake was conscious and in terrible pain; this thought reached out and consumed me.

I wasn't able to focus on anything I did; so I went back without telling anyone. The snake was still there, still twisting, but softer now, as if it was losing hope. My family's attempts to comfort me rang in my ears:

All creatures suffer.

It was just a snake.

This is life. Let it go.

Maybe all creatures suffer, but it was not 'just a snake.' Maybe this was life, but that didn't mean I had to let it go. I had made a horrible mistake, and I knew it, but I refused to accept that there was nothing I could do about it.

Watching the eyes of the dying snake, I made my decision, hoping, praying that it somehow understood my remorse. I went and brought the spade from our backyard; it was meant for cutting through gravel, and I hoped it was sharp enough for this.

I buried the snake I killed in a paddy field.

Grandad saw me crying in the backyard with the shovel at my side and immediately understood. The words he spoke to me that day have shaped the rest of my life: "You are the strongest and bravest person in this house today. You are capable of doing what is right, no matter how hard, and if you could handle that spade, you can handle anything."

My grandfather passed away earlier this year. His love and wisdom have made me who I am. His death reminded me of what I learned when I ended the snake's suffering: that death is a part of living. Life is precious because it ends.

Telling this story is my way of keeping him alive, of keeping the snake in the paddy field alive. We often choose to tell stories that make us feel good, but "sharing the bread of affliction," as Rabbi Lord Jonathan Sacks put it, transforms tragedy into freedom. My grandad continues to give me the strength to remember and share even the most painful experiences; he inspires me to share hope.

I am reminded of that every year when I visit the paddy field.

The Power of Unity
Alem Shaimardanov

[The names in this story have been changed in order to maintain people's confidentiality.]

I remember the day we were sitting on a school bus. Anthony and I were talking about our school work and plans after graduation. We were excited about our future and who we would become. I was saying that I wanted to study in the US and become a top finance analyst. Anthony was dreaming of pursuing a degree in Computer Science. At that time, we were thinking that nothing could stop us from achieving our goals. We just needed to work hard enough and that will be it. Later did I realize that hard work was not the only factor in making our dreams come true.

Anthony did not come to school for several days.

Teachers were asking me and my classmates if we knew what happened to him. His closest friends texted him, but he did not reply. Only a week after, his teacher informed us that Anthony was in a hospital and he needed to take a medical leave.

We were shocked. We asked the reason and the teacher said that Anthony was diagnosed with a brain tumor.

Silence...

We had no words to say. All I was thinking about was our school bus ride when Anthony and I were casually talking about our future plans and discussing school work.

All of a sudden, I realized that all our daily problems and complaints were nothing in comparison with what Anthony had to deal with. We took too many things for granted. We were making plans for 5, 10, or even 30 years in advance believing that we would have the same energy, health, and no unexpected situations. We may create our plans for the future but life may send us difficulties that we would never expect.

Brain cancer. I did not believe it. I remember Anthony as a strong and healthy young man. He went to the gym consistently and did not look like he was sick. Then I recalled that he was complaining about the pain in his knee, but he said it was because he was working too much in his backyard at home.

We asked the teacher if we could visit Anthony, but she said that was unlikely to happen. A few days later we were informed that Anthony's illness could not be cured in Kazakhstan. The best option for him was to get treatment in South Korea, but the costs of the surgery were enormous according to Kazakhstani measures.

Now, our main goal was to collect that amount of

money in the shortest time possible.

The student council had an urgent meeting with the school administration. Representatives of every class of our school met in order to discuss the ways of raising money for Anthony's treatment.

I remember how our class's WhatsApp chat was constantly active. We were discussing what kind of events we needed to organize to raise the money.

We came up with a plan - we organized charitable sales of students' artwork and pastries for the entire week. Our school was in proximity to Nazarbayev University, and we asked our school's alumni to organize charitable sales there too. Our student council asked the leaders of other schools within our. country's network to organize similar events and pretty soon our little fundraising event was happening nationwide.

But the main event I remember was the charity event at the city's popular mall.

Students organized a charity concert for Anthony's treatment. People played national music instruments and sang national songs. We were selling lottery tickets to the visitors of the mall. The winners received gift certificates from the fitness and beauty centers that agreed to help us raise money. My classmates sold their artwork and clothes. All the money that we had collected was sent straight to Anthony's parents' bank account.

After three weeks of active social media campaigns, collaborative work with other schools within our network, and partnerships with businesses and sponsors, we collected the necessary sum.

I remember how we all just smiled at each other when we heard this news. We hoped Anthony would get his treatment in South Korea and join us again. We were excited to speak to him again, like the old days, and catch him up on what he missed.

What touched me the most was Anthony's parent's reaction. They sent a video in which they expressed gratitude to every person who was involved in raising funds for Anthony's treatment. It was heart-touching to see the tears on Anthony's mother's face, but those tears were the tears of gratitude and hope.

In a month, Anthony had the brain surgery in South Korea. The surgery went well and with no side effects! Now Anthony had to undergo the rehabilitation process. The physicians said it would take around six months for him to get back to normal life. Although this was a long period of time, we were hopeful that Anthony would join us soon. His life was saved and that was the main thing.

// Comment: The image above was used during the fundraising campaigns for Anthony's treatment. The robot on the left symbolizes Anthony's passion for robotics and technologies. He participated in various robotics Olympiads and competitions. Letter 'A' is the first letter in Anthony's name. The image of the heart represents our love, compassion, and hope for Anthony's life to get back to normal.

The Value of Mentorship
Kacper Ścibski

During one of our meetings, we spoke about the ideal kind of mentorship. We unanimously agreed that everyone needs a mentor in their life. Those could be our teachers, idols, family members, religious leaders, or even peers. They are the people who guide and help us lay a foundation for great achievements to be built upon.

I immediately thought of all the important people in my life – from my grandmother who taught me how to pray to a friend of mine who had advised me to apply to NYU. Yet, JLF helped me to acknowledge the most important mentor for me – my mom. Thanks to her, I gained the greatest passion of my life – travel.

I think I was 14 years old the summer this story took place. At that point, I had already done some traveling with my family. We had gone to the Middle East a couple of times. However, those were just all-inclusive holidays in 5-star resorts – either in Sharm el Sheikh, Egypt, or Port El Kantaoui, Tunisia. We had also once gone to London. My mom and I visited a cousin living there. Our family took good care of us and showed us around the city. That journey to London was the first of its kind, as we spent the majority of the time sightseeing. I enjoyed it so much more than the luxurious hotels of the Arab world, that I made a resolution – no more tourist agencies! Next summer, at age fourteen, I came up with the idea of going to Paris – obviously without the comfort of having a tourist guide. Instead, I planned the whole trip by myself. I took care of everything that my mom would otherwise: flights, hotels, transportation, the itinerary, and a detailed budget. I took care of everything not because my mom wasn't able to, nor was she too lazy. I simply wanted to prove my maturity, independence, and planning skills. From a time perspective, I now know that my mom wanted to teach me all of these values by throwing me in at the deep end. I am extremely grateful for all the trust she invested in me. Since then, we have always been travelling together, sometimes to some of the most exotic destinations I could have ever dreamed of.

Indeed, our lectures were yet another kind of great mentoring I have received. In my opinion, universality and flexibility were the very precious features of JLF meetings. Our discussions always found a sense of common agreement between people of different origins and beliefs. Personally, as a Roman Catholic, I had a chance to revisit, as well as think of various aspects of faith and life. In addition, I learned much new about my "Older Brothers in Faith" – as we refer to the Jewish Community in my religion…

An Ironwood Shabbat
Daniel James De Beer

I don't come from a Jewish family, nor have we found any Jewish ancestry in our family records. I'm a South African who has never really lived in South Africa, travelling all over the world with my parents who are international teachers. I've called Korea, Madagascar, Mozambique, and now the United Arab Emirates, home. We're a Christian family, and are quite devoted to the faith, belief, and relationship with God. Everything revolves around Him in my home, and every decision my parents make is tempered by this fact.

For example, when I was younger and we lived in Madagascar, we'd pray every night before we ate, and my Dad would read from the Bible after dinner. It was so strange for me going to a friend's house and sitting at a table for dinner – I didn't know when I was allowed to eat. I found myself awkwardly waiting for someone to take the first bite, in the absence of the auditory cue that "Amen" would usually give me.

When I was around 15 years old, my parents brought a new tradition into the home, one that was in cultural very different from the Bible reading we did, but in origin in fact quite similar. My dad told us one day that we were going to start doing Shabbat. The word was strange to my ears, and I was quite awkward about it at first. We brought in candles, red wine, and bread, and after dinner on a Friday night my Mom would start it off. "Blessed are you, eternal our God… "After a few weeks, she'd forget some of the words and I'd fill them in for her."…ruler of the universe, who commands us to light the candles of Shabbat." She would light the candles – at first, they were a store-bought affair, but later my dad carved a beautiful polished dark wood holder for them, with three cut-outs in which to place them (*tamboti* or ironwood, it could have been).

My dad would take the bowl of broken-up store-bought bread, and continue: "Blessed are You, eternal our God, ruler of the universe, who brings forth bread from the ground." I would sometimes add, under my breath, a prayer inspired by the book of first Corinthians: "Thank you Lord for your body, broken for us." We'd each take a piece and chew slowly, in silent contemplation. He did the same with the wine: "…who brings forth grape from the vine." We'd each take a sip from the wineglass. Then my dad would get up and ask each of my brother and sister and I, in procession, whether he could pray for us. The prayers were of blessing, and it would come with a warm hand on the shoulder, his hopes and dreams for us spilling out like the wine we'd just drunk. Sometimes my little sister would ask to pray for my parents, and we'd gather around them and pray for them too. What started as a seemingly awkward appropriation became a stone in the wall that held us together as a family.

25

Short Trip Down My Mental Health Struggle Lane

Fatima Nadeem fn2039@nyu.edu

"Finally, Box number 4!". Packing the whole of my life at 'home away from home' in cardboard boxes and running to catch the bus sent me deep into the abyss of memories. The past few months were a roller-coaster of emotions. My hair was messed up, so was my head. Loneliness, depression, and tiredness were my bread and butter for the first semester of NYUAD, with the pandemic being the cherry on top. The thought of having to come back in few weeks overshadowed the emotion of happiness for going to my 'real home'.

Fast-forwarding with warp speed to next semester

because that's how fast time goes by when you are happy. With things going same as last semester, I was miserable now and forever. Coming from a brown family, the idea of self-care and mental health was never on the list of my known terms. Maybe they should have been. Learning in JLF about the practice of turning off electronics so that the people in the power station can rest convinced me to try it, turning off the 'workaholic Fatima' to find a 'Free Fatima'.

The process began with few walks on the Highline to just feel air serenade me; yes, those first few strokes do make one feel like they are in a fantasy world. From planning my day to complete one deadline after another, I started blocking out few hours a day for just doing whatever I wish at that moment. Never knew this would lead to catching the bus at the last minute for beach, malls and trying out random local restaurants in the city. Every passing day towards the end of the semester has made me realize the deadlines will always be there, life will always move on, all that matters is if the edges of your lips are pointed up or down.

The Beauty of Choice
Myriam Bekkoucha

Sheikh Zayed, the founding father of the United Arab Emirates is a man that has impacted my life in a way that may not entirely make sense. To my younger self, he was a man that was larger-than-life. A man with a vision, that saw skyscrapers where there was a desert. It was the 2nd of November in 2004 that I remember going out for a walk with my mother, as the golden sun began to set. My mother took the opportunity to tell me, "Mimi, Sheikh Zayed died." To my 4-year-old brain, I couldn't quite comprehend what that meant. What was death? Where did he go? As we returned home and I took a shower to wash off the humid air, I closed my eyes and saw darkness. This wasn't the usual darkness that one encounters behind their heavy eyelids- this darkness was the nothingness that I was sure death would be like.

It was from this day onwards that my extreme questioning of life began, namely: how should I live my life? I would seek answers from anyone and everything: books, old people, children, poems, experiences… It was also this continuous questioning that led me to sign up for the Jewish Learning Fellowship, yet another place where questions could be raised, and ideas shared. As we discussed Jewish philosophies and traditions, I felt myself inching closer to finding my answer. It was one source in particular that spoke to me. "Yehoshua ben Perachyah said: Make for yourself a teacher; acquire for yourself a friend; and judge every person on the positive side." (Avot 1:6)

This advice came to me during a time when I was feeling uninspired; I had been following my routine perfectly and lost the spontaneity that came with life. I had become used to spending all my free mid- semester hours in some form of academic development, learning a new language, catching up on my class readings, reviewing my assignments or listening to endless podcasts. I was following routine and could hardly say that I was living life. I was more so existing through my routine in order to achieve what I thought would propel me towards success. Oh, and after I reached this success would I begin to live my life more creatively. Yehoshua ben Perachyah's choice of using "make", "acquire" and "judge" were intentional. As I understood it, these strong action words prodded us to be deliberate with our lives. Once the class ended at 9:15pm Abu Dhabi time, I jumped into bed and reflected on this quote…How could I forget the privilege of choice? Choosing what to eat, choosing whether to work, choosing to listen to a genre of music, choosing to wear clothes that make me feel good or any of the other hundreds of choices I make in a day… Did I mistake my lack of inspiration for a lack of motivation? The answer was obvious, yes, I did.

Although my questioning hasn't relented, I emerge with one possible answer to how life must be led. It must be deliberate and appreciated, not only for the blessings that we experience, but for the friends and mentors that guide us along the way.

A New Sun
Maya Muwanga

"The world is ending in 2024." These words stopped me in my tracks. My fingers scrambled to rewind the podcast and hear those words again: "In the novel, the world is ending in 2024." I was on the side of a street outside campus and it felt like that moment when something blurry comes into focus. I was on a walk, trying and failing to plot out a running route for another day. I had been moving at a steady pace, listening for the first time in a long time to a podcast that I love.

The show's latest series featured individuals who imagined new futures for the black diaspora. This week's episode focused on Octavia Butler. Butler's science fiction was groundbreaking and genre disrupting, placing women and black people into a genre that had long been white and male-dominated. Butler's very being challenged who could write and enjoy science fiction, and what the genre could tell us about the coming times. 2024 is the year Butler's Parable of the Sower begins. 2024 is the year I will graduate from college. It wasn't always going to be this way. Life happened, I took a gap year, and my future was a year delayed. Except, I don't know if delayed is the right word.

Back when I grappled with my changing plans I found solace in the number twenty-four. Four has always felt lucky to me, so twenty-four felt ordained. I like round and even numbers. 2024 is beautifully round and even and then it ends in that blessed four.

I started college a year later and a world away from anything I could have imagined when I was younger, and as I listened to the podcast host's words it felt like I was clearly seeing what my new reality meant. I lived in Abu Dhabi. My memories of college would be set against this city. My immediate surroundings were barren and flat. Desert within a city within the desert. The glow of streetlights in the dark produced a setting any science-fiction writer could admire. How did I get here?

When I was younger I devoured fiction and fantasy books. I was a black girl in what felt like white Colorado, and at times my existence felt weirder than anything I had read. I felt simultaneously exposed and ignored; highly visible but never seen. I imagined far away worlds where my strangeness was marveled, where I lived a life magically different from my own. I was forever writing personal science fictions and years later I found myself on a strange planet, so alike and so different from where I'd come.

I have been thinking a lot about my past lately, trying to trace the course of my arrival to Abu Dhabi. For so long I forgot the adventures I once sought, and the way I embarked on my greatest adventure yet feels almost accidental. But if I take a step back, it is the only thing that feels right. Any other place wouldn't have been enough. Any sooner would have been premature. I don't know if I believe in destiny or a higher power. But I have often felt like life has a rhythm. Hindsight forms a path out of what happened, but I don't know what we would do if we couldn't mark those paths.

I have been thinking a lot about speculative fiction lately. What it once meant to me and what it tells me now. For a long time, my imagination felt limited and my mind felt tired and my future felt narrow. I'd forgotten how big and far experience stretched. How the alien can become home. Octavia Butler said, "there's nothing new under the sun. But there are new suns." More and more lately I've been thinking about new suns.

My Decision or His?
Eliza Mic

I always knew I wanted to study abroad. My dream program would be in the US. I knew that a liberal arts education would fit my personality and goals best. There was, however, this other part of me that knew my parents could never afford it. Even if I were to get the tuition covered there was no way my parents could pay for my living expenses on top of their mortgage and loans. This "realistic" part of me also knew that she had to go to med school. It was "the most prestigious and honorable job" as my dad would call it. I liked the idea of going there. It was only appropriate for a straight A's student in post-communist Romania. And so, I started to prepare for the med school exam in my junior high, taking bio and chemistry lessons.

I liked it at first until I started to realize that it was all about memorization and close to no logic required, not only for the exam but also in the next 6 years of med school if I were to get in. Biology, a subject I used to love, I soon started to dread and even feel physically nauseous when trying to recite all I have learned from the chapter the day before.

When I found out about NYUAD and the possibility of getting a full scholarship I got so excited. I immediately started telling my parents about it. My mom was already used to me coming up with another country I wanted to study in. She thought it was just a phase, I learned after some time.

My dad, on the other hand, asked me right away, "do they have a med school program?"

I said "No."

He immediately started yelling how I'm not going anywhere, how I was just daydreaming of useless travelling. He saw some of my recent Facebook posts shared from HONY where older people were encouraging the younger generation to take advantage of their youth and travel. He was so upset by the idea of not doing med school and potentially ending up doing a "useless" major like psychology or music or theater.

I left the house in the heat of the argument and joined my brother for his driving lesson. I was about to cry and called my biology teacher asking her for advice. She told me nobody should dread learning the material and that it was a sign med school was not the right thing for me. I came back home after midnight. I pursued my application telling my dad that I could still go for med school after I graduated.

Fast forward to 4 years after where I am about to graduate with a degree in biology, plenty of music and psychology electives and no plans to go to med school. My family came to visit me in my sophomore year and randomly met up with some of my professors who were praising me. They saw how much this university had to offer and how dedicated their professors were. A few days after that trip, my dad finally admitted "You were right, you made the right decisions...by accident."

Getting a Bit Closer
Mariana Lugo Celedon

We met in high school and since then, we have been the best of friends there could ever be. I would be there for Shahar when she had trouble sleeping and Shahar would be there for me when I felt overwhelmed by life. We had a true connection after bonding through indie rock bands and watching Brooklyn 99. Aside from our similar taste and belonging to the same friend group, Shahar also liked sharing her culture with me. Being a Jewish-Israeli of Moroccan descent, she had a variety of rituals and events that she liked to organize with the school community. By Purim time, Shahar and the rest of the Jewish community organized a dinner on our floor in which everybody wore a costume, played music, and talked about the experiences they had in common.

Even though Shahar and I were quite close and usually went to cultural events together, that Purim, she did not invite me to the party – which was fine with both of us. If you asked me, I was just a clueless person who did not know enough about the occasion to ask for an invitation.

Yet the food they were preparing seemed delicious and I was friends with all the people going. Regardless, I felt that I lacked the knowledge to actively enjoy the holiday with them.

Shahar was always a person that valued and emphasized the role of Jewish culture in her life, and despite our friendship, I never got to connect with that side of her. She always talked about the way family, community and empathy were part of her culture and religion, and I could see how that shaped the way she always treated people with kindness and respect.

It was not until I started attending JLF that I could truly learn the ways her upbringing, tradition, and empathy are unique to Judaism. Hearing Uri speak about how community gives a sense of protection and confidence was a teaching moment that helped me see through the historical and moral repertoire of Judaism. Moreover, by discussing and comparing Jewish values and holidays, I could connect personally with the ways culture and religion influence the way we perceive the world. The emphasis on community, resilience, and support resonated with my Catholic upbringing, in which solidarity and support were the cornerstones of our interactions.

Estelik
Aiya Akilzhanova

Thinking about re-experiencing the generational struggle – the idea at the core of the Passover – I cannot help but think about my home country – Kazakhstan – where millions of people suffered throughout the centuries. I cannot help but think about the part of our population that died of hunger in the 30s. What would have been different if their means of living were not taken away from them? Would we speak better Kazakh as a nation? Would I not wrestle in frustration every time I speak my mother tongue?

I cannot help but think about the brightest of our nation, the ones who called the nation to wake up from darkness and ignorance chanting Oyan! Qazaq through their art. The ones who fought for our autonomy, language, identity, which cost them their lives. What would they think of us now when all we do is shy away from who we are?

I cannot help but think about the soldiers fighting to the last drop of their blood in the 40s – yesterday's high schoolers called for war. They were governed by the desire to defend their land and their loved ones. They were never taught to kill someone on the battlefield and were never ready. No one is. Yet they fought and I am wondering how they felt. Did they think of their families? Their nation or land?

I cannot help but think about the students rioting on Almaty streets in 1986. Students who were younger than I am now, revolting against the government, confronting them. Protesting for independence after centuries of turmoil, confusion, and struggle. I wonder if I am able to do the same now.

It hurts to realize I am not. I am too weak, too afraid, too anxious. Stakes are too high, timing is bad, impact too low. It is when I think about those years and those people that I question myself and my stance. This memory engraved in my subconscious, while always somewhere at the back of my mind, awakens every year at the same time. I can't help but think of those times. Most importantly, that I can and will do everything for it to not happen again.

World History & Family History
Susanne Niemann

History – the translation of this word in my native language stands both for what happened before us as well as for the stories we tell each other to make sense of our personal experiences.

I also had a school subject called history in which I learned about the sociopolitical past of my country and the history of the world in relation to my country and as perceived from my country. These histories contain facts such as numbers, places, and names. But they also contain biases.

We cannot travel back in time so our understanding rests on the oral and written records of historians, time witnesses, and also our ancestors. Growing up, I loved listening to my grandma's stories - histories - of life, her life, when she grew up. When she was my age, just 21. When she met my grandpa at the bank and knew, even before exchanging their first words, that she would one day marry him. When she was pregnant with my mother and suddenly had to marry. When I was born in the blue house that we still live in today.

As a child, I took these stories and her excellent memory for granted, but now that she is growing older and I live further away and don't see her as often, I wonder, what will happen to those stories? Will I remember them? Will she be able to share them again next time I see her?

Last year, my grandpa passed away unexpectedly. He never told me his stories. I never asked him to. But I wonder what he would have told me had I asked him.

My life is closely linked to their life, their decisions to move places and change work, and the very coincidence that they met - both originally from a different part of our country. I am thinking more and more about creating an archive with the stories of my family. Stories of those who are alive. Stories of those who are remembered. Stories for those who come next.

What stories will I tell my children and grandchildren? And what are these stories made of? I find my grandma's stories so fascinating because the world changed so much during her life - from World War to a divided country to the Internet and her granddaughter studying on another continent while she did not leave our country until after marriage. Our stories – my grandma's, my mother's, and now mine – are made of people we love and care about. But also those who we let go. They are made of smells and tastes, of experiencing something for the first time, and something for the last time, of summer vacations, of flour spread on the floor by a toddler, of scarcity and abundance, of chocolate sent by relatives in the same yet not the same country, of oranges for Christmas, of clothes we held on to, and opportunities we let go, of being there for each other, and of learning how to give space to each other.

If there was a book of our family history in which every member would write something for the next generations — and maybe I will start such a book while my grandma still remembers her stories and is still able to write them down in her own words — I would want to write about the love and solidarity in my family. While we each pursue our own interests, and while our values might differ at times, each year on Christmas Eve we come together again at my grandma's place and there is a space for everyone.

In Body and Spirit
Cameron Wehr

I was born and raised in California to a family of Irish Catholics dotted throughout the state. My mother escaped her father's chiding and moved to the Bay Area where she found my father, and they created a family together in suburban America. My neighborhood was quiet, old, and fairly diverse, though everyone had some level of affluence relative to the national average. My parents raised me and my brother in a Catholic Church, attending masses on Sundays or Saturdays, driving us to Sunday School, participating in Bible studies and church music groups. Despite this, I always felt an estrangement with a higher being, a higher power in these large alters and open spaces. I bid my parents' wishes to appease them, but I waited until after church to get home to my usual video games, desperately awaiting a more material entertainment.

In high school, I had friends from all different backgrounds: Buddhists, Jews, Muslims, Protestants, Jains, Hindus. But I never really engaged with any individual one, in spite of this exposure; my experience with Catholicism and the rigidity of the Catholic Church soured my interpretation of religion and religious dogma. I deemed myself atheist to escape questions of faith. My queer identity further encouraged me to disentangle myself from the tumultuous religious homophobia that I struggled with throughout my childhood. From a distance, I felt I sense of false security—a position well-suited to avoid my donut-loving, pious grandfather.

I only became more open to the teachings of world religions when I started to listen to a podcast on meditation, which was a revelatory experience that showed me a sense of connection through spirituality, not religious dogma. I began to understand the appeal of religion and its teachings, beyond commandments and bound laws. It was a sense of community, connection, belonging—an engagement with others on how to perceive the world and act within it. JLF has afforded me this engagement, providing me the community with which to discuss and debate philosophical pondering and understandings of the material and immaterial world.

There is a curious sense of connection when others around you want to understand the processes with which we conduct ourselves and facilitate each other, a connection that religion often fosters because of its sense of higher order, something much beyond our corporal selves. In one such afternoon in JLF, we discussed the nature of discussion— redundant, perhaps, yet insightful. In articulating the means of community, we ourselves were creating a temporary community, senses of connection and belonging. In investigating connection and community, I myself felt a sense of connection with those around me. JLF has offered this opportunity to build community with those alike and unlike myself—in all of its arguments, disputes, agreements, awkward silences, intentional face expressions, and blank stares. Learning about Judaism was an opportunity to collectively reflect on my own identities and positions within the world and how religion and spirituality can enhance my everyday experiences. I remain hopeful for the future, and hope is a beautiful ideal.

Adapting to be Open
Phil Wee

When I first arrived at NYU, one of my biggest difficulties was to adapt to the environment. Not only was the semester my first on campus, but it was also the first semester I'd be able to meet my classmates and explore the city that I would call home for the next three years. To add to this, I didn't know anyone, so I was basically left on my own. I found this really challenging. Just a few days in, adapting to the life on campus pushed my body and my mind to its limits. I didn't know what to do and where to go, and since there was no in-person orientation because of the pandemic, it made it figuring things out all the harder.

When I arrived on campus, I didn't know where my room was—and when I eventually found my room, I realized I didn't know where to do laundry. When I felt hungry, well, there was always food in the D2 canteen, but it had a really weird taste compared to what I was used to—which was fine, but I didn't either know anyone to eat with. Back home meals were a key part of my day since it was the one time my family would be together and share our thoughts of the day. That made it all the more saddening to have weird and lonely meals.

These uncertainties and times of confusion compounded one after the other, and by the end of the first week, I honestly felt hopeless. There were nights when I would just lie in my bed and feel resigned to my tragic situation. I simply couldn't understand how other students survived and even thrived in this really different campus life. This was the case until I garnered the courage to ask an upperclassman I'd met in a class how they dealt with it. He gave me a lot of friendly advice and shared his experiences, but there was one thing that he told me which I have remembered until today. He told me: "It is really important to be open." This tip has allowed me to adapt to campus life much better. I started talking to my roommates, classmates, and even people I just met when I was walking around campus. I shared my struggles and heard people out, I've built a support system and got to know other cultures better.

After joining JLF, I've come to realize that my fear and close-mindedness had enslaved and shackled me from being able to grow. It was when I shared more about myself, when I became willing to open up and share with others, that I was able to bloom. Similar to the Jewish practice of seder, it is important that one is open with their hearts to grow in fellowship and faith. Being open and sharing more of oneself is what allows hope and true freedom to blossom in one's life.

Planning Time For Rest
Megan Marzolf

Recently, I have learned the importance of shabbat. Being on campus this semester, away from my family and partaking in four challenging courses, it became easy to be overwhelmed and homesick. It was really difficult to balance these feelings with all of the good ones I was also experiencing. I made new friends from Jordan, Indonesia, Shanghai, you name it. I swam with jellyfish in the Persian Gulf, explored the city, and ate new foods. Being in Abu Dhabi and being at New York University Abu Dhabi changed my life for the better in so many ways. But still, it was hard to explain how I could have one of the best days of my life one day and spend the next feeling engulfed by homesickness, calling my family crying because I missed them so much.

Through my Wednesday night JLF class I realized that a

big part of this fluctuation stemmed from over-scheduling myself. I felt pressure to make the most of being in the UAE. For so long I had dreamed of being in this country, and now I was finally here. I felt as though I needed to pack activity after activity into every weekend to make sure I was maximizing my time here. I joined the football team, and I got my scuba certification. I enrolled in latte art classes and toured the city by reviewing cafes. My Indian friends took me to Indian restaurants, and I trusted them to order me an unforgettable experience. I stayed up late having girl talks and woke up early to play tennis. I was having the time of my life, but it was not sustainable. This scheduling forced me to organize each day in my planner, sometimes making plans down to 15-minute intervals. I was exhausting myself. However, after learning about shabbat in class, I realized I needed to set time aside for rest. I realized shabbat would be a good practice to incorporate into my everyday routine. I needed to plan unplanned time. Time for rest.

Now, I use my morning cup of coffee to watch the sunrise and read my daily devotional. This is my shabbat. This time for rest allows me to set up a positive and peaceful mindset before my day really begins. I also push myself to do something active every day. Whether it is walking or playing football, I know that when I move my body it makes me feel better and sleep better. Since I started making time for my shabbat, I have started focusing on my downtimes instead of skipping them to cross more things off my to-do list. I now prioritize my rest through learning about the practice of shabbat, and I am very thankful that I do.

It allows me to focus on the best moments and prepare myself for more to come.

The Remains of War
Julius Grüner

I sit on the highest point of the roof. Before me, I can see the outstretched landscape of hills and valleys. While the chilly wind gently passes me, I enjoy the quiet and the break from the last few days. From up here, everything seems peaceful – but on the way here from the hotel, we drove by a mass burial site where hundreds of men were slaughtered in one night.

The remains of the war are everywhere, collapsed buildings, bullet holes in every wall, and from time to time, soldiers passing. The last days were not easy, survivors telling us how they lost their families and Austrian peace-keeping soldiers relating their struggles daily interviewing inhabitants to report the current tensions. The things that happened here in Srebrenica and being directly confronted with the palpable occurrences of history make me think. It appalls me what cruelties humans can commit even to their own neighbors simply based on one's ethnicity and religion. It also makes me realize how complicated conflicts can be, like for example in Srebrenica, how the international community was unable to properly react beforehand despite knowing what was going to happen. As these thoughts travel through my mind, I take one last look at the hilly landscape and while I climb down the roof I remember the value of our house building project – so that this does not happen again and the wounds of this war can at least be healed partially.

For me as an Austrian, growing up in Vienna and enjoying the quality of life of Western Europe, this trip visiting Bosnia for the first time truly showed me the downside of humanity. But it also reminded me of what great lengths people go in order to help others in need. Seeing what others have accomplished to flatten the tensions to restore a normal everyday life inspired me to be part of the process of establishing peace in the Balkans. So, I signed up at an Austrian organization to construct simple wooden houses for war expellees in Bosnia and a while later, I, together with three other adults made our way down to Srebrenica, where we were happily greeted by the architect and the future homeowner. The next few days we would get up by sunrise, drive through the valleys and hills to the construction site and spent the next 10 hours pounding hundreds, if not thousands of nails. It was a demanding time period, but I will never forget the grateful look in the homeowner's eyes the moment we handed him the keys to his new house. He also continued to smother every single one of us with kisses and to mark the occasion he even sacrificed one of his four sheep, which had been accompanying us during the construction time, for a celebratory feast.

Why our work mattered was because we would not simply give war expellees their homes back, but because it bounded people together regardless of their ethnicity or religion. During the construction phase, all the neighbors would come together and try to help in every possible way. One Bosnian neighbor came every day with a bottle of schnapps and while offering everyone a drink told us how happy he was for finally having his new neighbor even though the new homeowner was a Serb.

Being Israeli in the UAE
Michael Shiloh

When I started teaching at NYUAD, I was delighted to hear about study-away opportunities, including J-Term, and that our network of satellite campuses included one in Israel. Being originally from Israel, the opportunity to bring an NYUAD class from Abu Dhabi to Israel excited me tremendously.

However, as perhaps the only Israeli at NYUAD, I have never been sure how to engage in conversation about Israel. Indeed, I have my own unresolved questions: I deeply want justice for Palestinians, and at the same time am committed to Israel's continued existence.

I wonder too whether others feel similarly reluctant to speak about their homeland, such as students from Turkey, Iran, Qatar, or students of the Shia branch of Islam.

I am grateful for this JLF program in general for creating this wonderful community, but especially because the conversations we've had have shown me that there is the potential for these difficult conversations to take place on our campus. I invite all students with any questions about Judaism or Israel to ask me or talk to me about anything. I certainly don't have all the answers and will freely admit when I don't know, but I will do my best to find someone who does. I especially encourage difficult or challenging questions about Israel and Judaism.

Finally, my proposal for a J-Term in Israel was recently approved for January 2022, so I feel that my story has some resolution, in that what I dreamed of doing 4 years ago is finally scheduled to happen. I hope this is the beginning of many such study away opportunities from NYUAD to NYU Tel Aviv. I hope these will create strong friendly ties between Israel and Abu Dhabi, and students from all around the world.

An Open Heart
Sofija Jancheska

Shabbat, Passover, Purim, Yom Kippur... The House of Hillel and the House of Shammai. A few months ago, if I were to hear these words, I am quite confident that I would have to google them to find their meaning. Now that my JLF experience has almost come to an end, I am proud to see my knowledge growth not only about Judaism, but also about my ability to discuss life's big questions.

It was particularly Leo Goldberger's talk in class that pushed me to think about our sense of belonging. Leo was born in Yugoslavia; he spent his childhood in Czechoslovakia, Sweden and Denmark, and later immigrated to the United States. Yet, at the end of his talk, he said: "I am proud to be American!" This pushed me to ask myself: Where is home and what makes a home for us? Is it the place where our family is? Or is it the place where we feel the safest? Going back and forth with these questions, I concluded that the US was the place where Leo felt safe to continue living his life after all the horrors and sadness during the Holocaust. A place where he could start living a normal life, doing educational work about his people's history without feeling threatened because of his identity. And I also realized how fortunate he was. He was able to survive the hardest time in the history of his people without suffering as much as the six million victims of the Holocaust, and was able to eventually find his home. His story made me think what a journey it has been for everyone else, including my people.

Leo's story reminded me of my grandparents who also survived WW2. I never knew their exact birth dates because their documents, homes and villages were completely burned out. But, they were fortunate to not have experienced the horrors happening to their Jewish friends on the Balkans. When they were older, my grandparents also saw the Yugoslav Wars. The violent conflicts from 1991 to 2001 were quite a strong hit for all ex-Yugoslavian countries. But somehow, I was always hearing my grandparents, their friends and even elderly strangers in the public transportation on my way to school talking about their lives in Yugoslavia with so much love and nostalgia. Quite surprisingly, the topic of the country's breakup was never discussed in a hateful manner despite all the atrocities during the wars. It seems to me that the new borders might have physically disassembled these six new republics, but the hearts of the people have remained unified.

These open hearts of my people reminded me of Leo's. One would expect that he would talk with a sense of resentment after the most heartbreaking period for him and his family, but there was not even an ounce of bitterness in his words. When I asked him how we can help prevent the spread of anti-Semitism in today's world, Leo told me: "Treat everyone as if you do not know anything about that person, treat everyone like a human..." This did not seem to answer my question at first, but it later made me realize its potential to resolve the root of conflicts stemming from religious, ethnic and cultural aversion. We as young people have so much to learn from his words and from the words of all elder people who have understood that nothing can be resolved with hatred. Instead of investing our energy in having human beings against human beings for no good reason, we need to do our best to save the memories of our ancestors. To do our best to keep their experiences alive and inherit their open hearts.

The Cultural Contract
Adi Baurzhanuly

Connecting my personal story to a topic I've learned in the JLF class is not an easy task. In class, we have discussed all of these big ideas (or, how we might want to put it more fancily: *Life's Big Questions*) and I just haven't had any proportional events in my life related to these questions. Now, of course, I asked and answered different *whats* and *hows* about me and my culture, but I hardly believe that my Q&A was more unique or more interesting than that of other people. So, instead, let me consider *Life's Small Question*: what is NOT a culture? Just any example of it? Like, a desk, a pen, or... a dog? I would say that all of it simultaneously is and is not a culture to some extent and for a variety of reasons. Yes, I love being ambiguous. But I will provide you with clearer examples later on.

Beforehand, we need to give a "not culture" a proper name. Google suggests a list of antonyms for culture: "rudeness", "ignorance", "impoliteness", etc. That can't be it, right? These words don't do much for my essay, and yet I need to name the cultural superposition of my identity. Let's just go with "non-culture" – at least for now. So, we lazily define non-culture to be everything but culture.

So, what is culture? Or even more importantly, what is *someone's* culture? It is always hard to define and explain something totally spiritual and abstract yet at the same time something material and real (a desk, a pen, a dog, and so on…) But it is even harder to place it within your personality. Or place yourself within it.

Consider me. I didn't understand my culture very well. I tried to escape it, to become someone who is not a part of Kazakh culture. But after a lot of time and energy spent, I figured it is impossible to outrun your culture. It is not ahead, nor behind you. It is with you. It is in you. And more importantly, you are in it. I was "chained", and I wanted to break free. I changed my view, and I was free. Again, I love being ambiguous.

Now, I want to find a way to measure how much of my identity is explained by my culture. You know, how free I am. Or chained. Depends on where you are. For that, again, let's consider me.

I used to think that I do not need to enforce my culture on me. That it's a natural process – understanding and becoming a part of the culture. Manifesting, and exploring your culture. But after the JLF class dedicated to Passover, I figured that it might not necessarily be true. I learned that people recite the old stories of the rescue from Egypt to their children, and I figured there probably is a need for it. " *When one sees a spring, one should let it break through"*. A Kazakh proverb.

So, I used to think that "being obsessed with your culture" is a bad thing. It is harmful. But now I believe I was wrong. There is the harm if one brags about their culture. If one takes something impossible from it. Something that the culture didn't say, didn't mean. Now, that is my example of non-culture. Taking from culture something that it didn't mean. You can't change the amount of your culture in yourself. Or change the amount of you in your culture. Your chains don't get tighter or looser. They either disappear or not. Man, I *love* being ambiguous! But in a nutshell: exploring, questioning, reciting, and repeating everything you know about your culture is truly being free. Being free from judgment, from criticism, from fear. That way, you better understand your culture. And yourself.

People of the Book
Mayson Taylor

When my grandmother died, she didn't leave me much, just a stack of poems she'd copied out of books I had never read. At first, I looked at them with disappointment in my eyes, wondering why she hadn't left me money or antiques as it seemed she'd left everyone else in the family. I had actually had my eye on the painting she kept of my great grandfather's pub, the place where she grew up, and at age 16 met my grandfather, who would become her great love.

It took a few months for the grief to pass but once it did, I uncovered an empty space within me. An empty space where she used to be. I found myself wanting to know her for who she was, wanting to know her for more than just all the roles I had seen her play. This need was not just about her, it was about me. It was about knowing where I come from by knowing whose life made mine. I decided to ignore this aching feeling I had and thought I may as well add it to all the other aches I had being a university student spending most of my time with my neck bent over a laptop screen.

I'd dragged my grandmother's poems with their raggedy edges and yellowed papers halfway across the world to Abu Dhabi. As an international student, it is my habit to fill time with new information. I consider it my job to absorb as much knowledge as I can before they send me back home where novelty is a little scarcer. I'd enrolled in a morning class on the philosophy of personal identity, a midday class on the practice of creative writing, and an evening class on the intricacies of Jewish life. There wasn't anything connecting the three of them until there was.

In the Jewish learning class, they spoke of how written history is like a home. The Jewish people are people of the book. It is writing that creates a continuous community, a continuous sense of identity. Hearing this, I felt jealous – I didn't have any writing that made me feel this way. Then, one day after class I was searching for a pen in my draw and came across my grandmother's poems. She may not have written them herself, but she chose them. She carefully copied them, word by word and so, they meant enough for her to spend time on. I read them over and over searching for her.

I found someone who could be intrigued by a change in the wind and humoured by a careful rhyme. A little bit of that space within me felt full knowing she read those words, knowing there was a way in which she couldn't have lived her life without leaving these words to me.

Exploring the Meaning of Meaning
of Friendship

Elena Sepetovska

Just like all other human relationships, friendships can be quite complicated with tension and conflict at times. One of the most challenging conflicts in my life was when I realized that a friendship I had was no longer serving me nor my friend. I was always too emotional and scared of hurting someone else's feelings. And for me, friendship is one of the most enduring and wonderful gifts of being alive. However, as we grow, some friendships change and can even end after long periods of time. Yet in my culture, it is more acceptable not to mention the things that bother you with the friends or people involved. Hence, I've never felt that I should bring up what bothered me with my friend. I did not realize at the time that communication is key in all sorts of relationships, and even though many people hate rocking the boat, lack of communication is like poison to any relationship.

What I did instead was assume things about the intent of the other person's actions. In my head, blaming them was just a way of convincing myself that I was innocent. But no productive conversations start with blame, although lots of fights do. When I was younger, I assumed conflict was the result of unmet needs such as recognition, fairness, understanding, and security. Now I know that there are countless reasons why some of the strongest relationships can fall apart. And sometimes, friends meet and their friendship is successful because they are sharing common experiences and interests. As we grow and mature, friends that were once very close to us, may no longer be there.

Learning about friendship in JLF made me think about this old conflict with my friend from a different perspective. In the Torah, Yehoshua said: "make for yourself a Rav (a teacher); acquire for yourself a friend, and judge every person on the positive side." Reading this quote made me think about the existence of one obvious truth and definitive way or perspective. Engaging with Jewish learning made me reckon with the idea that there is not one obvious truth or one definitive perspective, as my culture often made me believe. Exploring these different perspectives teaches us how to be in a world that recognizes change and complexity. This leads to a sort of openness and curiosity toward different ideas and people who see things differently. The key to long-lasting friendships is openness to new knowledge, values clarification, and a search for meaning that encourages people to think beyond their everyday needs.

Preservation
Gabrielle Branche

For the past six months I've been working on my capstone project which explored the question, how do you preserve oral tradition? I feel like I come from a rich and multicultural society with so many beautiful stories to tell and yet they weren't being preserved.

Then I started JLF. One of our first sessions was about preservation. This session struck me. I don't think I'd ever recognized that certain cultures and religions put so much emphasis on preserving the stories behind them.

This may seem small but until the idea of preservation became salient, I had taken it for granted. I'm from Trinidad and Tobago and like many Trinis, I have a very rich genealogy. While I can trace my Indian ancestry all the way back to the ship which brought my great-great-grandfather,

I only have bits and pieces of my African heritage – even though that is my dominant ethnicity.

At the same time, I grew up and continue to be a practicing Catholic, which like Judaism also has centuries of detailed documentation. Nevertheless, I don't think I was taught the importance of this preservation. It was just part of my life. A privilege that comes with not having that part of my past disappear.

I don't think anyone's past should be erased. And yet many of us know so little about from whence we came. I am grateful to JLF for bringing the conversation of preservation to the forefront because knowing your past is a gift and should not be taken for granted.

I am now finished with my capstone project, but I acknowledge that this is just the start. I may not have had my past documented but there's nothing stopping me from picking up a pen now. Even though I am still trying to answer my research question I have found a solid starting point. How do you preserve tradition? By not taking it for granted.

Being 'Good'
Colin Robert Campbell

Growing up, I was raised a Bahá'í. I am not currently practicing, although throughout my life I have constantly been asked the question you are likely wondering yourself, what is Bahá'í? To answer your question, the Bahá'í faith believes in the unity and oneness of humanity. Bahá'í's believe that all of the world religions have truths within their religions and that the prophets in Judaism and Islam for example are indeed messengers of God – but that's beside the point.

As I was often probed with this question, it made me really think about what my religion meant to me, more so than what the religion stood for. I found myself repeating the aforementioned explanation, but with every time I felt as though I knew less and less of what my religion stood for and meant to me. Ultimately, I felt I was somehow a 'bad' Bahá'í since I was not able to explain the religion like others could – completely and in-depth.

Then in our JLF class, one of the facilitators said that in Judaism, or at least in some Jewish communities, there is the belief that "any Jew is a good Jew". This idea really stuck with me and made me realize that it was not just specific to Judaism. Defining 'good' based on one striving to be their best within the guide of their religion rather than on actually succeeding to follow every practice seemed to me to be a much more attainable and realistic definition of what it means to be Jewish, or a Bahá'í.

During one of our classes, a guest speaker and Holocaust survivor, Leo Goldberger told us of his experience going to Germany some years after the Second World War. He spoke of how he felt frustrated and angry after an interaction with a German border officer. Looking back on that experience, Mr. Goldberger realized that his emotions had nothing to do with anyone but himself. He alluded to the idea that we are only in control of ourselves. Thus, we choose to be 'good' **Bahá'ís or Jews by striving to abide by our faith's teachings,** rather than by fitting the framework which has been given to us by others.

The Chicken and the Eagle
Thais Alvarenga

It was extremely difficult for me to come up with something to write for this project. I felt that in the vast expansion within my mind, no story that I came up with was good enough: writing something about my life felt weird in the sense that I didn't know what experience I should tell, and narrating a made-up story felt too easy and too broad. Since I was young, stories have always been important to me so I wanted to write something I would be proud of. After spending much time pondering the matter, I finally remembered the reason why stories are so important to me: because they teach us lessons, and I learn best when I listen to stories. When I was young, my parents would tell me bedtime stories, or parables. They each had some takeaway which I felt I've internalized very deeply, precisely because of the way I learned about them. Thus, I've decided to share with you one of the many parables that live rent-free in my heart. I can't remember the name of the story itself, but between us, let us call it "The Eagle". I pray that you will find some use in the teaching that it gives:

Once upon a time, there was a man who, while walking through the woods, found a harrier. He took it to his house and put it in a coop. Soon the harrier learned to eat the same food as chickens and behave like them too. One day a naturalist who was passing by asked the owner why an eagle, the king of all birds and birds, had to stay locked in the corral with the chickens.

"Since I have given him the same food as chickens and I have taught him to be a chicken, he has never learned to fly," replied the owner. He behaves like a chicken, and therefore he is no longer an eagle.

"However," insisted the naturalist, "he has the heart of an eagle, and, with all certainty, he can be taught to fly."

After arguing some more, the two men agreed to find out if it was possible for the eagle to fly. The naturalist gently took him into his arms and said: "You belong to heaven, not to earth. Open your wings and fly".

The eagle, however, was confused; he did not know what he was, and, seeing the chickens eating, he hopped up and joined them again.

Undaunted, the next day, the naturalist took the eagle to the roof of the house and encouraged him by saying: "You are an eagle. Open your wings and fly". But the eagle was afraid of himself and the unknown world and hopped once more in search of the chicken's food.

The naturalist got up early on the third day, took the eagle out of the coop, and carried it to a mountain. Once there, he lifted up the king of birds and encouraged him by saying, "You are an eagle. You are an eagle, and you belong to both heaven and earth. Now spread your wings and fly."

The eagle looked around, toward the corral, and up, toward the sky. But he still did not fly. Then the naturalist raised him directly to the sun; the eagle began to tremble, to slowly spread its wings and finally, with a triumphant cry, he flew off into the sky.

It is possible that the eagle still remembers the chickens with nostalgia; It is even possible that, from time to time, he will visit the corral again.

Let no one know, the eagle has never lived a chicken life again. All along, he was an eagle, even though it was kept and domesticated like a chicken.

I Choose to Remember
Zerina Rahic

In the history of humanity, there has been no natural disaster or catastrophe that could compare with the horror of what humans did to each other. One of the most brutal, inhumane acts done by people has been slavery. To take someone's most basic right, most important right, right for freedom. To wake up and decide that someone's life is more important than others is an event in history that we should all be ashamed of. But no human anger and brutality could ever compare to the mercy and power of God who decides whose freedom belongs to who. And therefore, the Egyptian enslavement of Israeli people couldn't break their spirit, their hope, and their belief that God will indeed set them free. During JLF sessions, I learned about Passover which commemorates the Biblical story of Exodus — where God freed the Israelites from slavery in Egypt. During the duration of the holiday, it is forbidden to eat leavened food products.

I find practicing Passover extremely important because it allows people to show their respect and put themselves closer to their ancestors. The people who fought and survived in order for future generations to live and be free. Despite that it is impossible for a free man to feel what slavery does once it puts chains on body, mind, and spirit, having a holiday that allows people to remember and express their respect through sustaining from food, in my opinion, is where the beauty of Passover lies. It teaches us to forgive but never forget, to practice but never repeat. It teaches us that no matter what we are going through, it is all God's plan. Therefore, I learned that Passover is not about the process of fasting from certain food, it is about keeping the memory alive among us.

On the 11th of July, every year without exception, my people, my family, and I do something that keeps the memory of my country alive. People of my country haven't been enslaved but recently they have been victims of one of the cruelest massacres in 20th century Europe. In July of 1995 during the Bosnian War, 8000 men and boys have been victims of a genocide that took place in the small town of Srebrenica. They tried to kill every man in that city and then continue into other cities to pursue their aim of ethnic cleansing. But my people never lost hope and belief that God will save them, and he eventually did. Therefore, on the 11th of July, each one of us puts a white flower on our chest and goes to Srebrenica and we pray for mothers who lost their husbands, brothers, and sons. We pray to God for it to never happen again, we offer forgiveness, but we never forget. And this small ceremony and practice helps us keep the memory of people who were killed so we can be free today.

Passover and Bosnian holidays might be celebrating the freedom of different people, but they both allow us to respect, remember and celebrate freedom of humanity.

Here is Where We Meet
Anna Rygielska

The city Wrocław, where I mostly grew up, has a long history of changing affiliations. In the past, it was German, Polish, Czech, and Hungarian. A famous historian of Eastern Europe claims that since its founding it was known by over 50 different names. Bresslau, Wrocław, Presslaw, Wretslaw, Vratislav and many more.

Its Polish name, Wroclaw, freely translates as "a glorious return" or perhaps "a famous comeback", which looking at it from the perspective of history seems like a manifestation of an exceptionally dark humour.

Polish people returned (?) to Wrocław after several hundreds of years in 1945 as part of the border change after the Second World War. Most of the people who replaced the German population of the city were refugees from the

Eastern part of the country, a vast majority of them from the city of Lview. It seems to me at times as if the whole city decided to relocate itself to a different place while keeping the social structure and local culture unchanged.

From the stories I have heard, for years people's lives in the city were defined by the feeling of temporality. Most of the Poles who had arrived in the late 1940s took over the homes vacated in a rush by their German inhabitants. The belongings of previous owners remained stored neatly in the attics and basements with the expectation that someday they will return to collect them. But for the most part, they never did. And now it seems absurd to think that they might ever come back.

But still, some do come. Perhaps to collect the scattered childhood memories of a period of time that got left behind along with the porcelain service and silver cutlery. Most cities in western Poland share a joke about retired German tourists who swipe through "our" streets in groups behaving loudly and commenting on what used to be there. Absurd experts of imagined geographies.

The city that they speak about does not exist anymore, though its remnants can be seen in the occasional dilapidated storefronts calligraphed in German on old townhouses. But neither does the old Lview that my ancestors sought to transport and preserve.

I think that for contemporary Wrocławians, the insecurity of having to vacate the city has mostly been replaced with the frustration of not being able to fully own it: not seeing the reflection of its "Polishness" in the architecture of the old city center or the history of the land.

But, my deep hope is that we will continue to evolve and one day we will grow enough to embrace our incompleteness; a result of living on the outskirts of the country, where the national identity becomes less pronounced from the constant exposure to the Other.

Leave Room to Fill
Hannah Kasak-Gliboff

More and more, I find that wisdom is the ability to live with contradictions, and, when having to choose between competing perspectives, to be able to come down on one side. A glass that is half full, will always be half empty as well.

For many, religion is a tool to navigate contradictions; a tool to choose which side to come down on. For others, religion is the supplier of contradictions. Describing myself as half-Jewish, I learned early on, was not usually a satisfactory answer. I grew up with religion at arm's length and never felt that it was missing from my life, choosing unconsciously to come down on the side of a glass half empty. Even so, I did recognize beauty in faith and the need for frameworks, stories, and texts to explore as a community. Because behind even the simplest of observations, there is a decision.

The School of Hillel says that a bride should be described as beautiful and graceful. The School of Shammai says that she should be described as she is, beautiful or not. Both are beholders of another person, taking in their own subjective impression of flaws, strengths, and weaknesses. The choice then presents itself in which perception – one of beauty or one of lameness – we choose to legitimize with words. Observing beauty becomes a choice.

We're faced with a similar choice in spirituality. You may be given the same moments in a day – moments of hurriedly trying to catch the bus, moments of quietness when you wake up just before your alarm – but what we attribute to them is a choice.

When I hear a church choir harmonizing and building up a major chord, I know what people mean when they feel spiritual, when they feel close to their god. And yet, I don't come down on that side. To me, a moment that feels spiritual is a moment of deep emotion and connection to myself, but not to a higher power. I understand and I value the spiritual; I understand and I value the glass-half-full approach; I understand and value the beauty in every bride. Finally, I understand that there is a choice in the side I come down on. We are not born into the School of Shammai or born into atheism, or born into a world of half-empty glasses.

In writing my story, I felt that I ought to deliver a message of inspiration. I felt that I ought to say "I saw half-empty glasses and spiritless-moments and lame brides, but that now I see the opposite." But truthfully, I've learned to see both. I've learned that at times it is best to highlight the positive, the spiritual, and the beautiful, but that does not mean losing sight of the other side.

I've become comfortable with the prospect of

contradiction, not just as a state of transition between two perspectives, but as the perspective itself. I've found more meaning in being half-Jewish than in clinging to binaries. And though it's a position difficult to explain, I've found that half-empty glasses have more room to be filled and that the honesty of lameness holds beauty in itself.

Take a Break
Abhay Menon

Too often our desire to succeed limits our ability to make ourselves a priority. Too often we believe that taking a break means losing time and will slow us down. As a bioengineering major and a premedical student, I believe I am no different. Stress, frustration as well as hard work, and passion tend to overlap and occupy most of the time of my day. However, at one of the sessions in JLF, I learned about something that seems so simple and essential but so hard when implementing it in practice. Shabbat - the seventh day of the week, the day of rest. The day when our wellbeing is our priority, and the day when time and world are allowed to slow down. I wonder how such a simple and logical approach is uncommon in our community. Maybe because technological advances made us so dependent on others: what are they doing, letting them know what we are doing, or maybe we are trapped in the mindset that if for one day we rest the whole world will collapse.

When discussing the topic of Shabbat, I expressed my worry that as an overthinker, I am scared that if I take a day just for myself, enjoying nature, reading the book, writing, all I will be able to do is overthink about all the things I have to finish for either my academic work or personal struggles. But instead of just listening to my concerns, one of the JLF facilitators told me that Shabbat is not about being lazy and unproductive in your room but instead it is about prioritizing yourself and your wellbeing through a way you believe it is the most effective. For me, this was essential to hear, and after the session, I was able to make a plan that would include one day a week just being for myself.

My own personal Shabbat happens every Friday when I go play basketball. When I play, my body, mind, and spirit become one. The whole focus shifts on the next move I will make, on handling the ball at the right speed, being unpredictable, and scoring. Basketball allows me to rest my mind from worrying about things I have to finish, rest my body from work and it allows me to restart and come fresh into the next week. Despite that basketball is not a passive process, but instead, it fills my blood with adrenaline, it pushes me just above my limit and what my body can handle but it still enables me to devote the entire time only to myself, the court I am on, winning mentality and one goal - not missing the shot. Learning about Shabbat allowed me to have a day in a week that belongs only to me, where every worry disappears, and I am fully committed to myself.

For Me, About Me
Elen Asatryan

I was walking down the streets of London. It was cold. It was lonely. They say that one in two thousand people have a superpower: they can see colors in numbers, taste emotions, smell names, and even hear the cities. Synesthesia... I am one of those superheroes.

London sounded like Beethoven: there was something charming, perhaps even sad about each and every breath of its notes, but the entire composition was too much to handle. Don't get me wrong, I love London, it was a place of interesting discoveries for me, about me. As I was living a typical student life there, I felt blue. Not sad. Just blue. I quickly came to discover that I am capable of accomplishing great things, such as scoring the highest in class, writing an amazing research paper, attending over 5 extra-curriculars, not missing any political conference or a mathematics Olympiad. That's not all: I could sleep 4 hours every day and devote the rest of my time to studying and perfecting myself. Perfection. That's how an A+ felt for me. My life turned into a formula 1 race, accompanied by the wondrous melodies of the 9th symphony. I couldn't have felt prouder about expanding my academic horizons at such an exponential rate. But something didn't feel right. It was getting too blue.

I was walking down the streets. It was hot. It was lively. The city sounded differently now, it was Tchaikovski, Waltz of the Flowers. People looked friendly, buildings welcoming and the sun beaming. It is quite spectacular how you start appreciating things the moment they are gone. And even more spectacular when the appreciation comes from the fact that those things are finally gone.

The recent pandemic has put an end to my "Formula 1 racer" career, where every grade mattered, and every minute was counted. I had to go through all five stages of grief before I could open my eyes to the new, yellow world that was awaiting me. Even more quickly than before did I realize that I am capable of accomplishing extraordinary things, such as meeting sunsets with friends, taking care of my body, practicing mindfulness, living in the moment, and spending time discovering my true self. Perfection. That's how mental freedom felt for me. As I was enjoying my ice cream in the park, hidden in the shadows of skyscrapers, I time-traveled to London, to my past self. Surprisingly, there was nothing I wanted to change: till this day I am thankful for the experiences, sometimes sleep-deprived, that I had as a student there. I am eternally grateful for winning my own race against myself. But I liked feeling yellow more. Yellow made me feel the warmth I was deprived of. And now, being the mature person I have become, it is time to set off on a journey to the crossroad of yellow and blue. Green is waving at me, as I am walking down the streets of Abu Dhabi.

And I feel happy.

And I feel alive.

True Connections
Andrijana Pejchinovska

Laughter bounced off of the walls. I was sitting on the couch next to my suitemate, and across from us was a friend and her boyfriend. We were chatting about high school and sharing (quite hilarious) stories about our past classmates and friends.

As we took turns telling stories. My suitemate described a vacation that she had with her friends. Something felt off in the whole story – she described it in abundant detail and told things that were highly unlikely to have happened.

Later on, I talked to her about her story. I questioned some things that she had claimed happened when suddenly she broke down crying. She said that she felt that pressured to tell a funny story because we all had interesting experiences and she felt that she had nothing to add to the conversation.

My suitemate has previously described her high school experience as "sheltered." She thought that she hadn't experienced much of the things that typical high schoolers experience because her parents were quite strict. So, she felt inadequate in the gathering and tried to make up for it by creating a story that she thought we'd find funny.

We talked about her high school experience and about the pressure to conform to college life. At NYUAD, we all come from different backgrounds and have severely varied experiences, yet somehow, we manage to create connections between ourselves. These connections can sometimes feel repetitive – you say your name, your major, where you call home, and an interesting story. And sometimes we feel like we have to go above and beyond to make ourselves interesting and stand out, especially among such brilliant people around us. My suitemate felt that same pressure – and told a white lie to fill in was what was missing from the conversation.

Conversations, however, aren't about proving how unique or interesting a person is. We already know that we are unique individuals, and what we really need is to form connections. These connections can not be created on top of lies and made-up stories – at the end of the day, connection is about creating something real and long-lasting. White lies can get you so far, but once you start to get to know a person and their past, white lies can not only stop you but destroy the connection that you've built with another person.

Experiencing Shabbat
Daniella Aruina

It was one of the first Saturdays during my study away semester in Tel Aviv. We got together with some other NYU students and went to a park for a picnic. Although it was a really nice experience and we had some interesting conversations, after an hour or so, I started feeling anxious. I had a few deadlines coming up and I was not spending this time working. I tried to get myself back to the present moment, but to be honest, it was quite challenging.

This was one of the first times I experienced Shabbat in my life.

The next Saturday, my friend and I decided to go to another part of the city to explore Tel Aviv. Little did we know that all public transportation was not working on Saturdays. Although at first, I was a bit disappointed, I asked myself — what can I do to make the best out of the probably not the most comfortable experience of one of my first Shabbats? This discomfort was most likely caused by the fact that I had not really been used to stopping for a bit and not rushing almost 24/7 in pursuit of deadlines/goals/events, etc. So I decided to take this sense of discomfort as a chance to learn how to take a step back, slow down, reflect, and be present in order to appreciate this beautiful tradition.

This was not an instantaneous switch of course, but rather a gradual process. Every Saturday, I would make an effort to do things outside of my "to-do list" or sometimes not even do things, but simply be. Be fully present in doing something that fills me with energy, such as reading a book, taking a walk, hanging out with friends, calling my family. Over the course of my semester in Tel Aviv, I realized how much I have learned and grown because of the process of simply "being", rather than "doing" something on Saturdays.

Now, the tradition of Shabbat has become my personal tradition, since every Saturday, I make time to take a step back, reflect through writing and meditation, and spend time with people that I care about by hanging out in person or talking over a Zoom chat.

The Possibility of a Peaceful Coexistence
Sudiț K. Sahoo

One thing that really motivated me to think beyond conventional ways and encouraged me to build bridges between communities engaged in conflict was when I began to understand that there are dangers in attaching a significance with past traumatic events. In class, as we discussed the vital role the remembrance of the Holocaust plays in defining Jewish identity, we were asked to discuss the possible impact of overly relying on historical narratives. I could not help but connect with my childhood experience, listening to my grandparents' stories of the partition of British-colonized India into the newly independent India and Pakistan and the widespread violence and unrest that followed. It is considered to be the largest mass migration of people in the history of mankind with millions displaced, killed, or just plain missing. The trauma of their memories shaped a particular image of British and Pakistani identity in my mind.

Through my interactions with classmates and other community members who identify as either British and/or Pakistani, I realized that unfortunate events that took place decades ago should not affect our perception of an entire ethnic group. I realized that co-existence and communal harmony are very much real and concrete possibilities.

It's pretty interesting that my curiosity to learn more about the Jewish faith led me to rediscover and acknowledge the feasibility of these prospects. The Jewish Learning Fellowship helped me develop a deeper sense of understanding for religion in general – apart from the specifics of Judaism. It made me realize that religion is much more than mere rituals. Through analyzing religious texts and unraveling their deep meaning together in class, not only did I receive an overview of the underlying metaphors in certain texts, but also the greater life purpose that they drive us to achieve.

And as I write my particular personal story, it seems that religion also promotes creativity by driving us to generate a fresh perspective of the present without being influenced by the past. It just goes to show that religion can be perceived differently as well. Usually seen as restrictive or rigid in terms of acceptance, religion is also a chance to rethink, and redefine our reality. ,

It shows the breadth of discussions that took place in our class and how critical thinking was promoted as we were motivated to share our opinion of the most fundamental events in history even though debating such matters could be pretty controversial at times. It was such a delightful experience to watch our classmates present their diverse opinions while being extremely respectful and cognizant of others' views. Moreover, my personal story goes a long way to highlight the importance of intercultural dialogue and I can not think of a better platform than the Jewish Learning Fellowship to engage in the same.

Don't Cry Over Spilled Popcorn
Dylan Herman

With every step, a soft crunch echoed from the bottom of my soles; each crunch marked the crushing of another leaf, breaking it apart, spreading the distinctive autumn reds and yellows across the empty grey parking lot. The pieces of wilted leaves added beauty to the otherwise dull scene, and I made snow angels in the crushed leaves before my grandpa impatiently ushered me to the cinema's front door. After purchasing our tickets to Shrek Forever After, we promptly took our seats, and to this day, the scene continues to resonate in my mind: the fuzzy, fake-velvet texture of the budget movie theatre seats; the speakers booming with pre-movie advertisements; and loud mumblings of a packed cinema.

Together, we sat, waiting for the movie to begin, and because the theater was packed to its brim, people awkwardly shimmying past us felt like a constant. For minutes people passed us, in and out, as we waited in anticipation for the feature film. Finally, as the advertisements were coming to an end, the theatre erupted with a rush of movement as everyone scurried back to their seats.

It was not until then that a woman hurriedly pushed her way down the aisle, caught her foot on the rug, and nearly fell on her face. Fortunately, she caught herself and regained her composure without a scratch on her body. Unfortunately, the same could not be said for the parcels of snacks she was carrying. As her body jerked back to regain balance, she launched an extra-large tub of popcorn directly onto my grandfather's chest, and the woman looked at him with the eyes of a deer caught in traffic, anticipating the rant of an angry old man. Instead, however, my grandfather slowly looked up to her, placed a piece of popcorn on his tongue, and told her, after a moment of consideration, "it needs more butter." Thus, with only level shoulders and sharp wit, he ended the interaction without anger nor scorn.

I often find myself thinking back to this interaction. Not only does it remind me of the character of my grandfather, but it also reminds me of a valuable lesson: to approach life with humility. Rather than seeking out all that is negative, take the opportunity to approach each moment with humor; put a positive spin on the mundane and frustrating. This is a sentiment that I believe that the JLF echoes: to treat others with respect and to respect ourselves enough to overcome our negative visceral emotions.

Galentine Goodbyes
Harper Cho

It was, all things considered, extremely silly.

It was Valentine's Day, and a few friends and I were feeling particularly lonely. Sad were we, students from all over the world washed up on a desert island with nothing better to do on a day all about love. So three sad single friends and I went out, bought a bottle of wine, five different kinds of cheese, boxes of crackers, and called it a board game night.

The incident began at around 8 PM exactly. Casey, who was my closest friend out of the three, came over early. Our game night wouldn't start for another two hours, but we were bored and a new episode of drag race had just come out. We were big fans of the show and would watch it every week without fail. This time though, we decided on a whim to invite another friend, Jess, to watch it with us. Jess was part of our little group of friends, but she was very much not single and had a boyfriend who we presumed she would go back to for a lovely evening date. So when the show finished, we said goodbye to her and prepared to meet with our other single friends for our Lonely Hearts Club. That was our mistake.

It seemed inoffensive to us at first, of course, but the fact that we didn't invite her to our sad board game night had apparently infuriated Jess. She was so angry, she wouldn't even tell us she was upset. We had to hear it from a friend of a friend. It was so petty, and to us seemed so small, we couldn't believe it. I laughed it off. I thought we'd give it a week and she would cool off and everything would be fine. I didn't realize we didn't have that kind of time.

The next day, late afternoon, I got a call from Casey to meet her outside in the back of the school. I thought we would talk about how silly Jess' reaction was. It wasn't that. Casey got a call that morning from her parents. Her father was seriously ill, and it's suddenly gotten much worse. She's already bought tickets to go home that evening.

It all happened so fast. The packing, the preparing, the late-night run to the supermarket to buy extra packs of masks, hand sanitizers, and gloves. All the while, I couldn't stop thinking about how our last semester only just started. We were meant to make memories as best as we could given everything happening around us. Instead, we were already ending it short. I felt like I was being robbed of something.

It wasn't until I was standing outside the school at two in the morning saying goodbye to my friend for the last time that I remembered why Jess wasn't here to say goodbye too. She stopped reading our texts and obviously couldn't have known.

That was crazy to me. We had all known each other for four years, building our small community far away from home. Oddballs who, in any other universe, would never have met. Our own little breakfast club. For a long time, we were all each other had. We all just wanted to find someone to relate to, to be close with, in this alien land. Yet here we were ending it all over something so silly.

I suppose that's why I wanted to share this story with you. In participating in the Jewish Learning Fellowship, I thought a lot about community. What it means to share something with someone and belong to the same group. What it means to identify with other people and establish bonds. What it means to sustain those bonds.

The next day, I baked cookies. I invited Jess over and we talked. Not about anything that happened, mostly about cookies, but it was a truce and that was something.

A Journey of Learning
Vera Petrova

I remember myself stepping foot from an airplane that just brought me to my next destination. A destination I never thought I would be able to come to, but most importantly stay for so long.

It was not only a new chapter in my life lingering on the edge of a new page of the book, but it was also fear and uncertainty of turning over to this page. I, as a Christian Russian, came to a Muslim country, miles away from home, with mosques outnumbering churches, with cultural aspects and ideas that in my culture and religion were normal, but here they were either different or uncommon. If you can imagine Nemo in that scene when he loses his father in the terrain of the diverse sea inhabitants and waves – that was me, lost…however, hopeful for new beginnings.

And new beginnings did happen! The journey might not have been as smooth as the surface of a well-mowed British lawn, but through the process - I learned. I learned how to listen, how to ask, and how to accept differences even though I might not relate to them. The international community that I have been exposed to here in Abu Dhabi, helped to broaden my outlook and realize that even with different backgrounds in religion and culture we can still have a conversation going.

That is why joining JLF: Life's big questions was the next step for my personal growth that I decided to take on. Jewish culture was always a topic that I had heard of. Back home many members of our town were of Jewish descent, however, I never wondered to ask them how it feels to be living in a place that does not necessarily celebrate their culture… JLF classes on Thursday evenings contributed a lot to my understanding and dispelled some biases I might have heard or seen. In addition to that learning about this religion and culture with my international students had made me realize how each of us accepts and understands nuances of it in a different way.

Giving all the political context that going on around us in the Middle East, it was very useful to step back a bit and dive into the historical roots of the Jewish-Arab relationship. Through my experience at NYUAD, I had the chance to mix with so many cultures, religions, and nationalities and I no longer feel like a stranger anywhere I would go…Things might be different, but that would never bring me the feeling of alienation. I learned that listening, accepting the fact of diversity, and asking questions in order to get out of the tiny box that at some point in life we are raised in is the key forward. Freeing our minds from stereotypes and miscon-ceptions is like outgrowing old clothes, they do not fit us anymore, so we stop wearing them.

My Shifting Sands
Andrew Platonov

Who am I? How do I fit in? Where am I going in life?

I was only 14 years old when my mother died and I was orphaned, which shocked me to the core if it wasn't for the fact that I didn't know that she was dying. She never told me about her illness. Her friends had to reveal the truth afterward: she was first diagnosed with cancer when she was 18. Radiotherapy saved and prolonged her life. The doctors, however, told her never to give birth as that would've affected both her and her child's health. It was only hers. My Mother was 51 years young. Was that bad parenting or her way to triumph over death?

Years later, I understand and marvel at some of her key decisions – her legacy gifts. Keeping her declining health a secret was one of them, her gift of not knowing. Instead of counting days till her demise, my mother wanted me to have the best possible childhood while she was still in control. And so, I had one, innocent and carefree. As my mother wasn't the last person in the city administration and was well-connected in many circles, I was accustomed to a certain lifestyle. I was very spoiled and had everything my heart could possibly desire. Although I saw that she was sick, I always thought that it'd be temporary, that she'd get better. Was I so blind to see the obvious? Was that wishful thinking? Was ignorance my way of dealing with death? It wasn't like my first time witnessing it though. Three years before, my grandmother died from a stroke. And it wasn't the last time either. Three years after, my grandfather died from a heart attack. And that's how my family was finished, my circumstances were reduced, and I was left alone.

Physical, psychological, and financial abuse that I later suffered from my legal guardian, who was my mother's cousin's sister, damaged me further even more so. That guardianship arrangement saved me from an orphanage, but not from cruelty. No coming-of-age story, after all, would be complete without a wicked stepmother figure. While there were other suitable candidates from the extended family for my guardian's role, my mother, for some reason, deemed fit that particular aunt, so questioning her decisions was not an option.

I had no options. Whenever there's an anniversary, I cry not because of missing my mother, but because of remembering what occurred after her death. Everything that I am, everything that I am not, is because of what happened that day and ever since. Do you know what kept me standing through all those tumultuous years, full of angst and uncertainty? No, not faith. Having witnessed so much loss and suffering, I had no faith left. It was school.

Another key decision by my mother was to give her one and only son the best possible education, her gift of knowing. I wouldn't be writing in this language if I hadn't been transferred from a standard elementary school to a school with advanced curricula in linguistics and foreign languages. When the time came to further specialize and choose your major for senior high school, I asked my mother for advice and, without any hesitation, she replied: "Do what you want to do". A month later, she died. Fully aware that I would honor and follow her choice, rather than mine, after her death, she gave me freedom instead in the most non-prescriptive manner. Studying was my respite; it became my way to escape my grim surroundings. As my guardian worked in Moscow, while she was away, I was left to my own devices. I'd do anything to avoid being alone at my own home, the same apartment where my family died, or not alone when the aunt was back "disciplining" me in all sorts of ways. So, I pretty much "lived" in high school, attended all available extracurriculars, and competed in all subject Olympiads. I was a good student before, but, because and in spite of my circumstances, excelled beyond any expectations. That's how I earned myself a scholarship to study at NYU Abu Dhabi.

The University was an escape in and of itself. I finally had options. There's no such thing as too much freedom, but, apparently, there was for me. Academically, I changed my major a few times - Political Science, Chemistry, Mathematics, Economics. Professionally, I worked at research labs and non-profits, consulting, and oil companies. Spiritually, to understand firsthand the varieties of

Christianity and Islam, I journeyed to Syria, Lebanon, and Iran; to experience Buddhism, I traveled to Nepal – amongst numerous other places. College is thought to be a perfect time for self-discovery. However, instead of finding, I lost myself more than ever.

As the last surviving member of my family, I burdened myself with a lot of responsibility. As I wasn't living up to either my own or other people's expectations, I developed a lot of self-loathing. I hated myself partly for the things I did or didn't do, partly for who I am and am not, and partly for my lack of imagination. I couldn't picture there'd ever been a moment in time or place when I could be true to myself or, at least, figure out who that even is. In addition to that, I didn't complete the grieving cycle, as one by one, members of my family had been dying with a three-year interval before I even started the University. Death is so terribly final, but it was unimaginable I'd ever attempt to end all my possibilities in life. I was tired. No family, no attachments, no love – who'd miss me? – I reasoned. Ironically, this failure of imagination is the one that saved me. I needed time away from academia to resolve my identity crisis. Now, I had to escape by going back to where it all started, I had to go home.

Only 10 years later after my mother's death, I finally managed to find closure – visited the cemetery, where my family was buried, and started properly living at my ancestral home – or so I thought. As I was browsing through family archives, I discovered my mother's final gift. I had always assumed I was just Russian. There was actually so much more. Old papers and photographs revealed that my grandmother was from Odesa – Not only am I also Ukrainian, then, but Jewish as well. I wish I could have asked them why they never shared any of that with me, but, understandably, the harsh realities of Soviet life made everyone blend in. Because of Soviet discrimination and coercion, everyone became "Russian" for the sake of pragmatic survival. Wearing a mask became the norm, and after wearing it for so long, people forgot who they were beneath it. At the time, there were other things to worry about than these identity politics. As unwilling participants of the "grand" Soviet labor experiment, my family had to move around the country a lot. According to their marriage certificate, my grandmother from Odesa, Ukraine, tied the knot with my grandfather from Oryol, Russia, in Temirtau, Kazakhstan; my Mother was later born near Luhansk, Ukraine. Soviet honorary certificates and awards helped to explain their mobility: my grandfather used to build towering blast furnaces as part of coal mining and coke production initiatives for the Soviets. Mapping those locations connects them to the areas with the largest coal reserves in the former Soviet Union: Karaganda coal basin - Temirtau, Donetsk coal basin - Luhansk, and Moscow coal basin – Tula, which is famous around Russia for its arms production, but, also, where I was born.

With my entire family dead, all of a sudden, I had this freedom to decide whether or not to reclaim the identity that had long been lost. This gift of choosing appeared exactly when I needed it, or perhaps when I was ready for it. For quite some time, I've been desperately trying to fill that irreplaceable void in my life with meaning and service, but to no avail. Questions of identity, however, never really mattered to me until Russia annexed Crimea and I became political. I couldn't stomach and buy into state media propaganda, so I had to see things for myself. Despite pleas from my friends not to go, that I would get imprisoned or killed as the Russo-Ukrainian War was still ongoing, I moved to Kyiv for a year. Not only did I gain a better understanding of the current events, but I also learned how they were related to past events. The history I knew was a little bit different as I came face to face with the politics of memory.

After the Revolution of Dignity, a large-scale campaign has been launched in Ukraine to revise its history, define its place in the world, and envision the nation's future — that resonated with me as I was striving to achieve the same but on a personal level. After all, any collective memory is formed and influenced by individual minds. But Soviet legacy is deep and pervasive. Is it ever enough to remove all Lenin statues, Soviet symbols, and monuments? Many critics see decommunization as an attempt to substitute a Soviet narrative with a new one, often influenced by the current political discourse. So, how do we deal with the complicated and troubled history of a nation or just our own? Is our narrative truly set?

I reconnected with my Ukrainian roots while living in Kyiv, but still had no idea what to do with my Jewish heritage. It wasn't until I joined JLF when I was presented with the opportunity to explore what it means to be Jewish and how to follow Jewish traditions. JLF helped me realize that there is the legacy I inherit, the legacy I live, and the legacy I leave behind — and that, most importantly, neither of them must be identical to one another. In fact, it never really is. The legacy we inherit is nothing compared to the legacy we leave behind, but the legacy that we live is playing the role of being the link between generations and is often overlooked. I lost everyone and everything, and yet somehow took up my family's mantle without even knowing what it meant. I'm done running from my past and keeping my story straight. I've been wandering my entire life and it's about time I left my desert. But if there's more (gifts) to be found, I'll keep wandering on…

Oh, The Places You'll Go
Bar Tenenbaum

This is a story that demonstrates how sometimes in life, the one door that you bravely decide to open leads to another one and so on, until you get to a place that feels like a peak, and that's when you realize you have unlocked the way to constantly reach wonderful places. This is what I have experienced in the past 10 months as I transitioned from working as a lawyer in a big law firm in Tel Aviv to MBA student at NYU Stern. I reached a peak while teaching sharp and curious students in NYU Abu Dhabi about Judaism, philosophy, and culture, and discussing their inspiration, aspirations, challenges, hopes and dreams. To reach this peak, I had to open doors from and into places I could have never imagined before.

If I had to pick one point where this journey began, I

would choose August 20th, 2020. I have a rare, sweet spot for this specific date. It marks a day, a few days after I'd left my job as a commercial litigator and a few days before I'd packed my bags and left on an airplane to New York, excited to pursue my Master's in Business Administration at NYU Stern. More specifically, it was a casual bright and sweaty summer afternoon in the center of Tel Aviv. I was just about to get a haircut in a chic hair salon recommended to me by a friend, when I suddenly received the call – or, as I call it here, my first door into the wonderful peace building opportunity in the Middle East.

Why the Middle East?

Well, as you may or may not know, a few days before that date, on August 13th, the Abraham Accords Agreements were signed between the UAE and Israel. It's not something I specified earlier, because honestly, as I was getting a haircut on that sunny day, it was the last thing on my mind. I was so excited and preoccupied about my final arrangements before leaving for New York that when I arrived at the first door, I was not sure I knew how to open it.

It was Lior on the phone. Back then he worked at an NGO called Israel-is that I'd connected to through a workshop of theirs for prospective Israeli MBA students abroad (Let's call that Pre-First Door). "Bar, I have an amazing opportunity for you," he said. "Israel-is is leading the very first forum led by 20 young leaders from the UAE and Israel, ten from each country". "Sounds interesting," I said, but I wasn't entirely sure what it had to do with me. Then, Lior said: "We thought it would be great if you were one of the 10 Israelis in the forum. Will you be interested in participating in the very first meeting that is going to be covered in the media today at... actually in about four hours?"

My heart started beating. I somehow felt, already at this moment, that this was the beginning of something big.

"I will be there at 7pm" I said, then asked the hairdresser to make some nice finishes and ran back home to begin my research. Reading for the first time about a neighboring nation of people I have never encountered before was fascinating to me and I was filled with curiosity and hope that this is the beginning of a new order in the Middle East.

At 7pm, on Zoom, was when I first met the people that very soon became my true friends and partners. After getting to meet the wonderful Emiratis that welcomed us with amounts of respect and love that were almost overwhelming, I truly felt at home. As if they were our close friends for years and as if the only thing that differentiated us was the religious hat that we wore. Naturally, those continuous connections have strengthened and have expanded into a large network of young leaders aiming for peace.

A few months later, as I became more involved in the emerging relations between the two nations, I participated in the Emirati-Israeli Youth Circle led by Rabbi Sarna, the Official Rabbi of the UAE, with the purpose of opening avenues for dialogue and understanding how to create a path forward and break down the barriers that once existed. It was in this meeting when I decided to knock on Door Number Two and reach out to Rabbi Sarna to introduce myself. I knew he was the Executive Director of the Bronfman Center for Jewish Student Life at NYU and the Chief Rabbi of the Jewish Community of the UAE and as a Student in NYU, I wanted to find ways to collaborate. I did not know what his response would be but after knocking on that door he immediately opened the door wide and kindly replied that he thinks we can work on great things together.

One of those incredible things was teaching the NYU Abu Dhabi JLF class of 2021 along with Uri, Jake, Sarah(X2). Rebekah and Rabbi Sarna.

Today, after 4 months of leading important and open discussions with the students in the class who expressed just the same amount of curiosity and sensitivity towards Judaism as they did towards their own culture and religion, I cannot imagine these 4 past months without them. Just as I was full of hope after meeting my Emiratis friends and witnessing their willingness to connect, I became even more hopeful after meeting each one of the students and noticing their sensitivity and openness.

One motive we focused on in class was the importance of learning from each other, including from our students and mentees, a true principle in the Jewish tradition. I am grateful for being aware of how much I learnt from my students through their insights and creativity in real time. The doors I chose to describe in the story are just two out of so many I have opened and will open in the future. And it is amazing how even just those doors have changed my life for the better and brought me to a true peak.

Made in the USA
Monee, IL
07 July 2026

56551483R00073